NATURE

MINDFULNESS MEDITATION ADULT COLORING BOOK

ASSEMBLED BY
MADDIE MAYFAIR

ISBN-13: 978-1537762739

ISBN-10: 1537762737

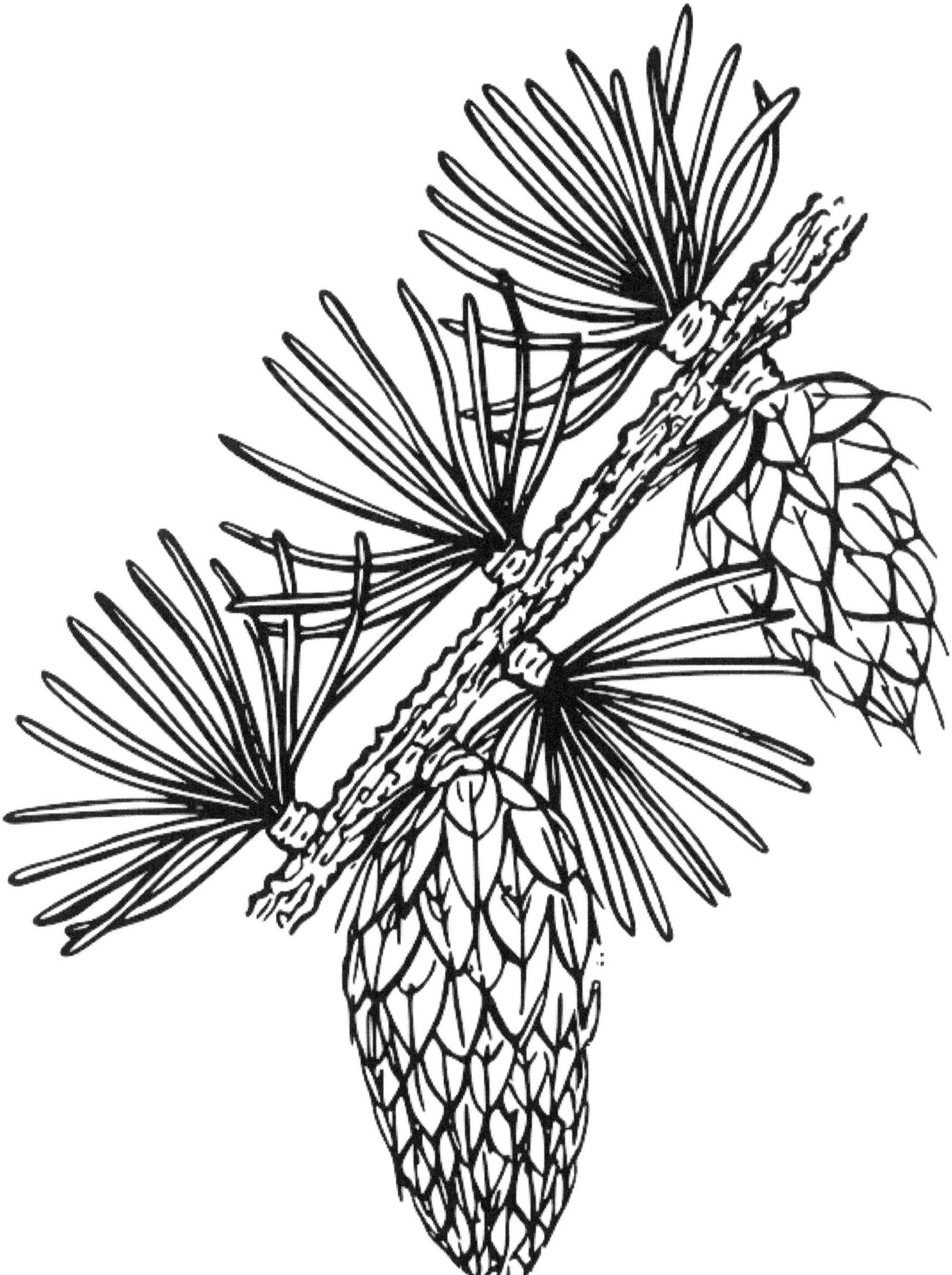

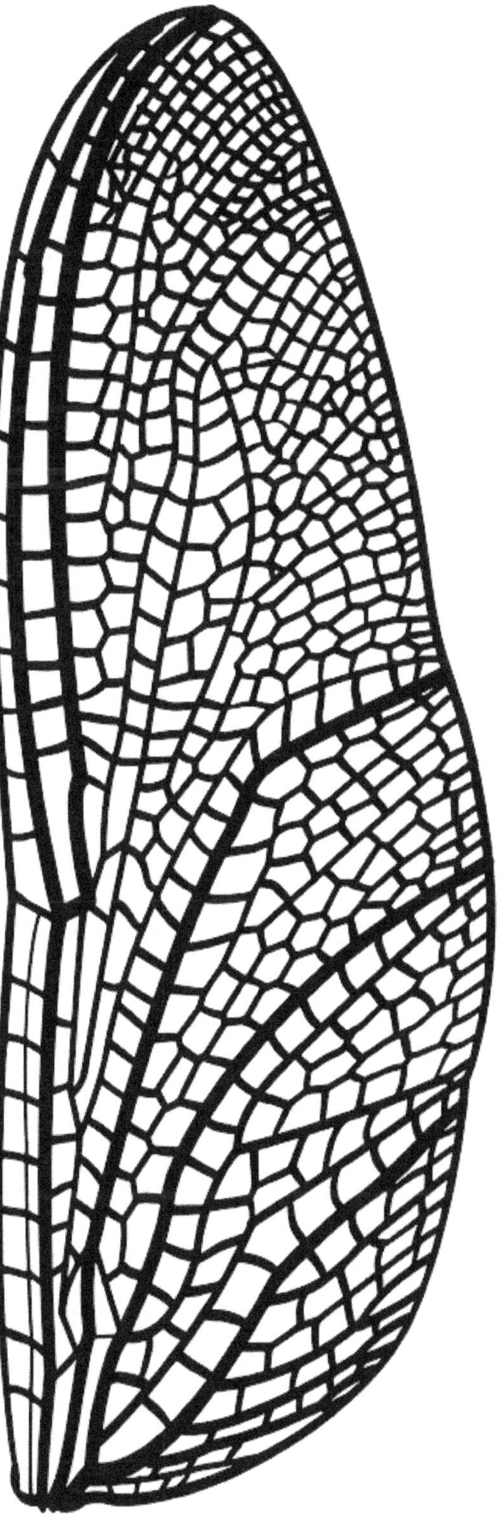

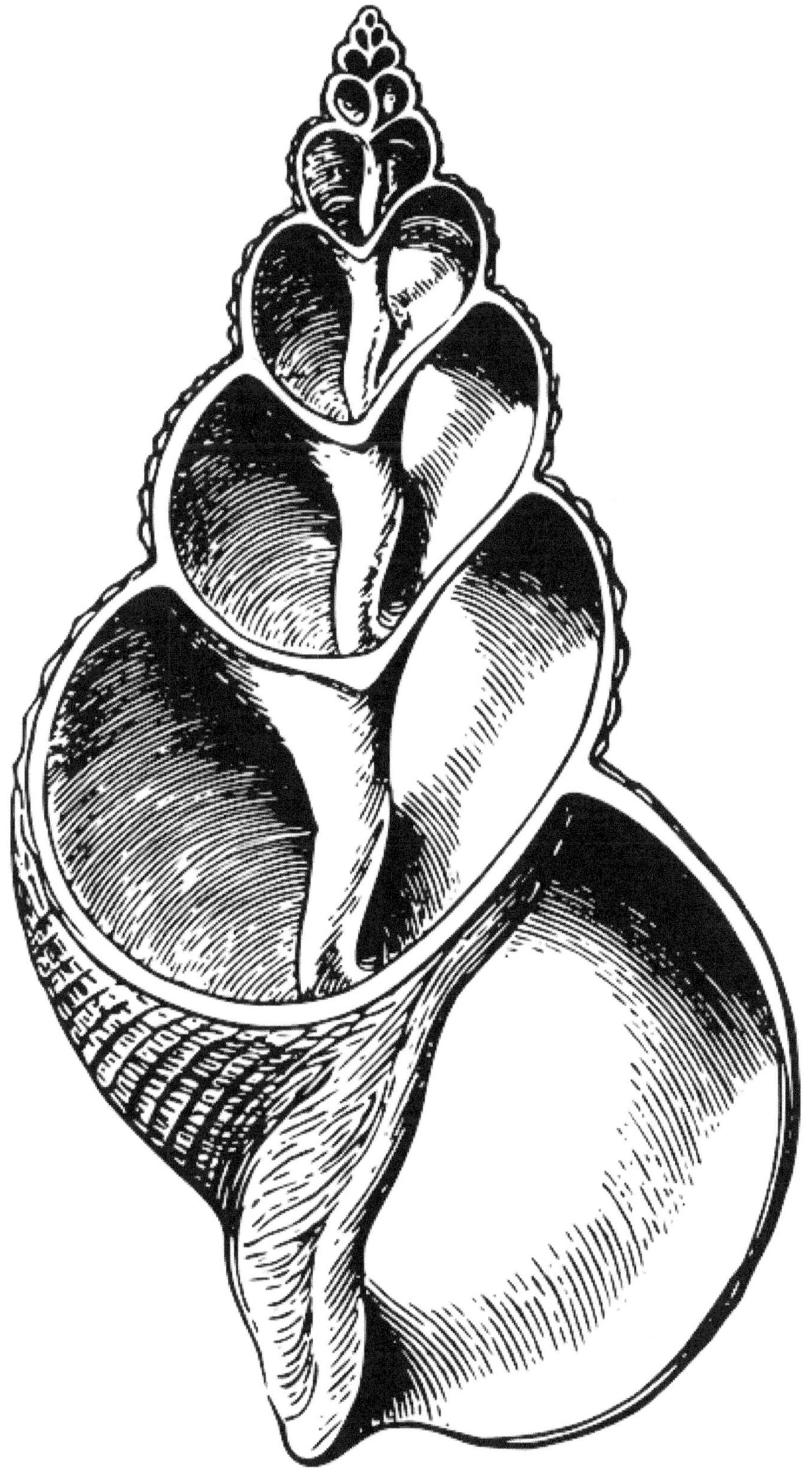

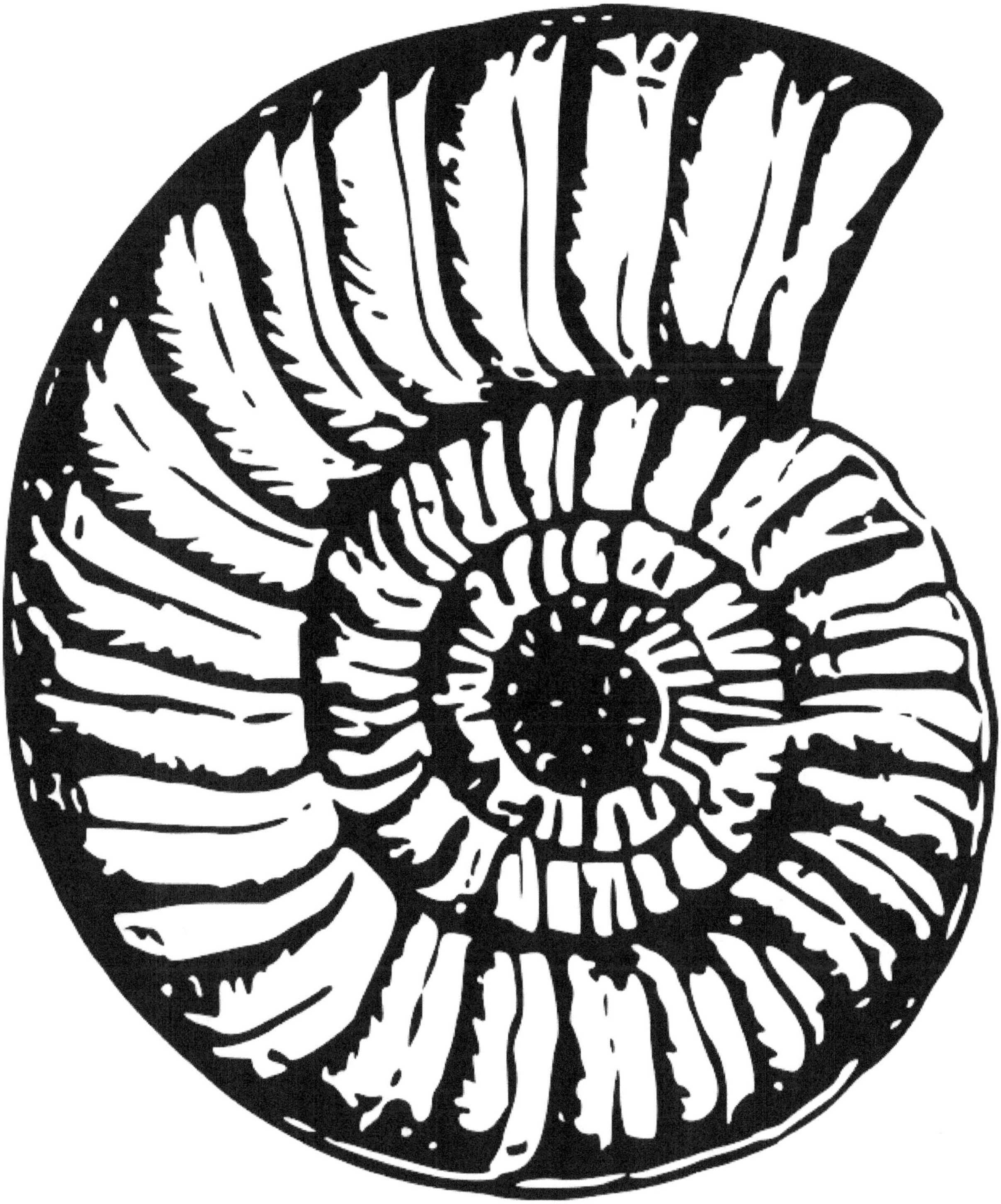

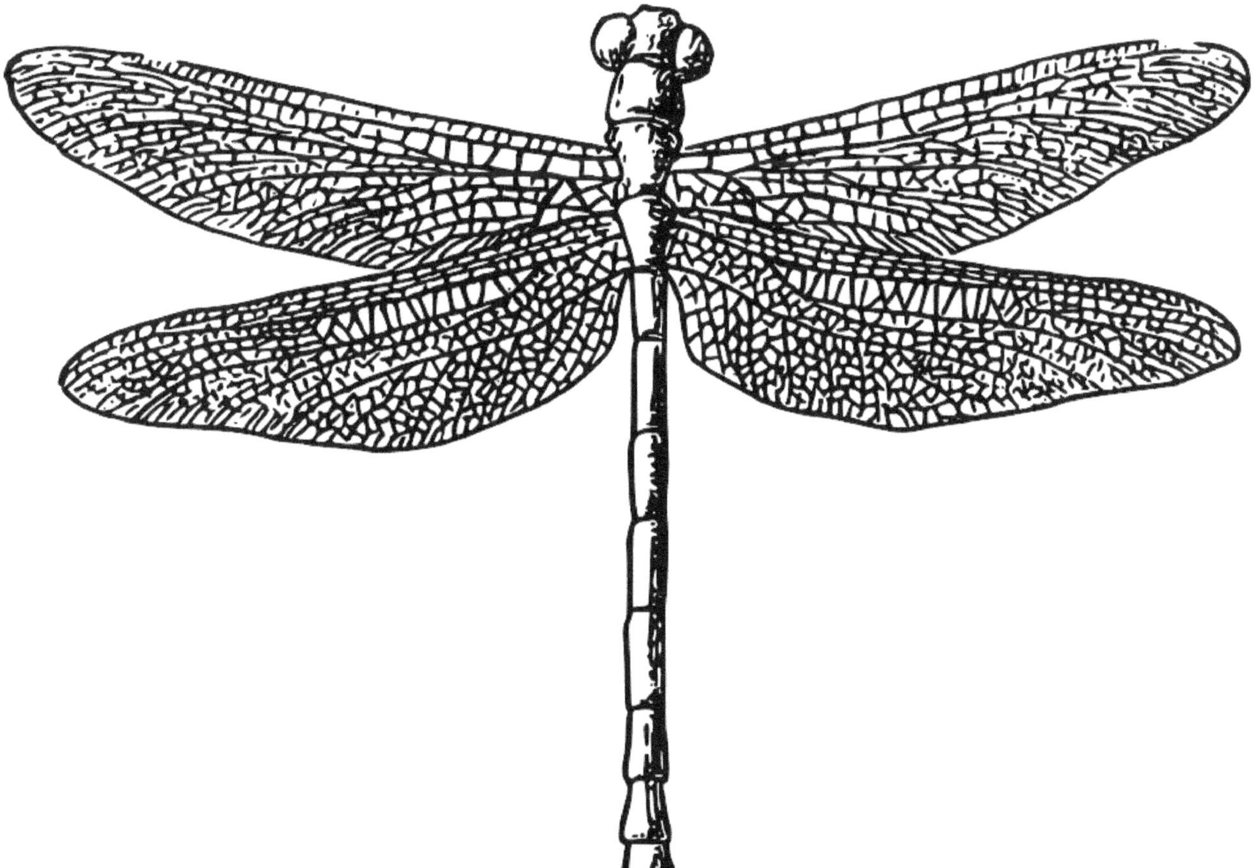

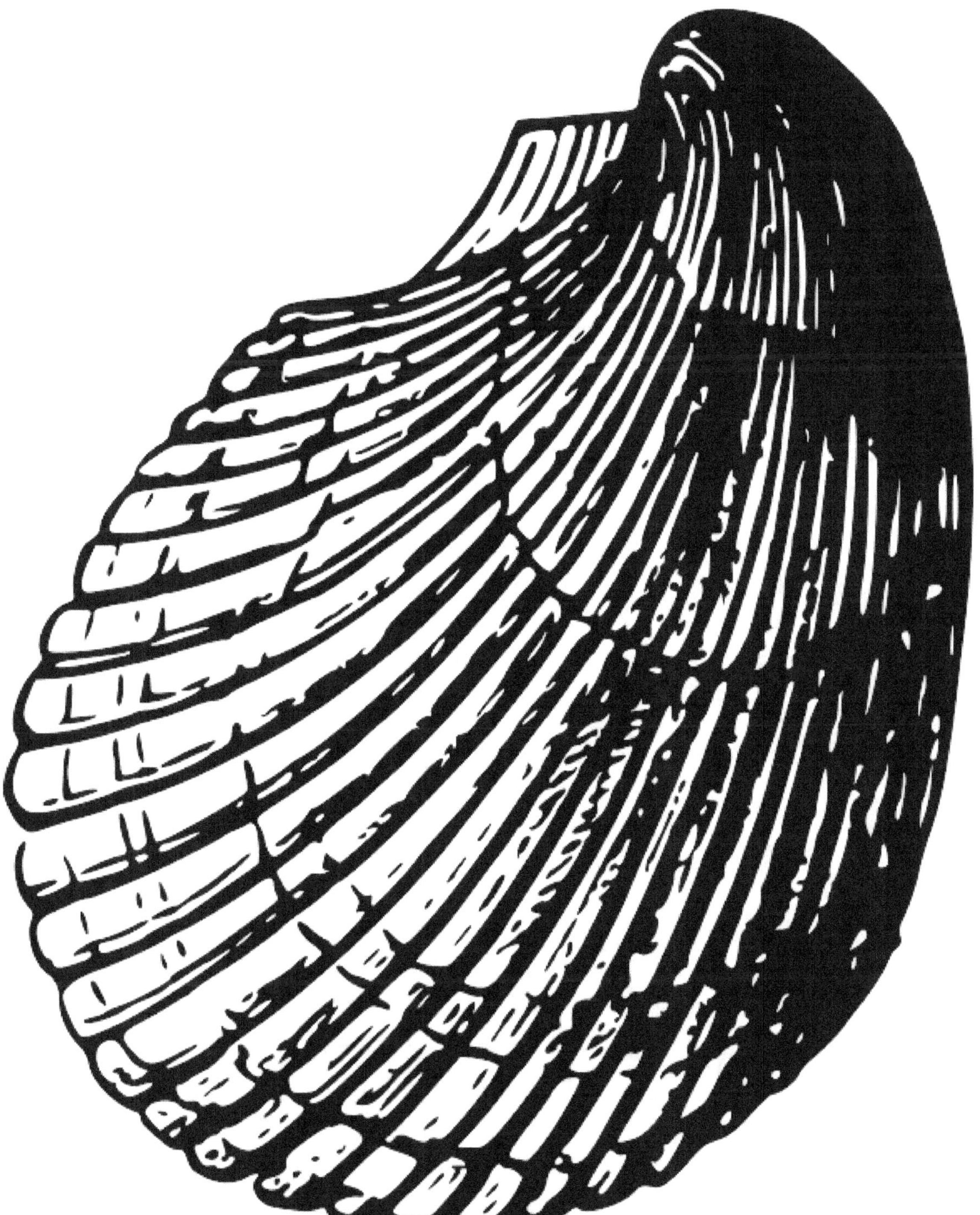

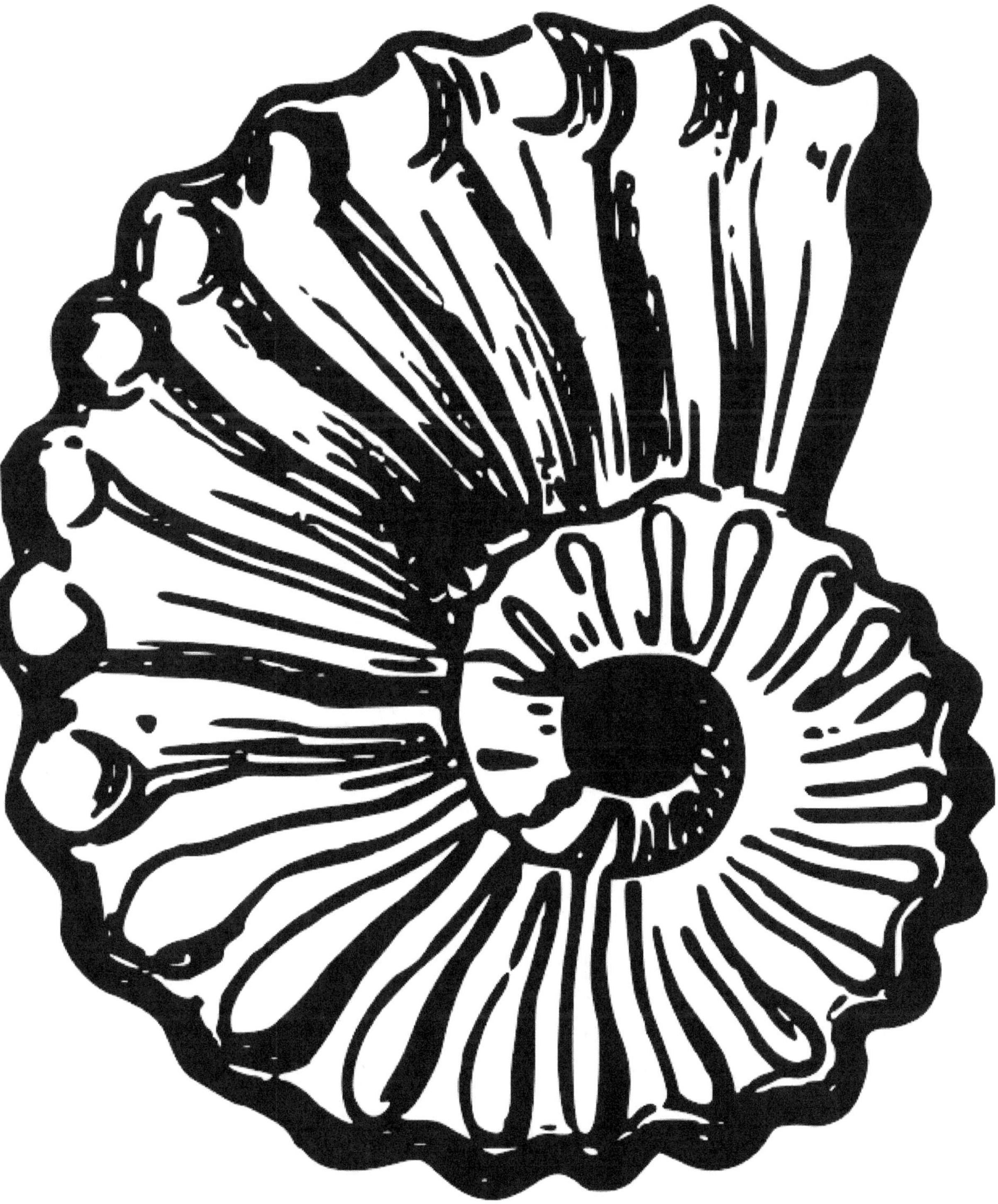

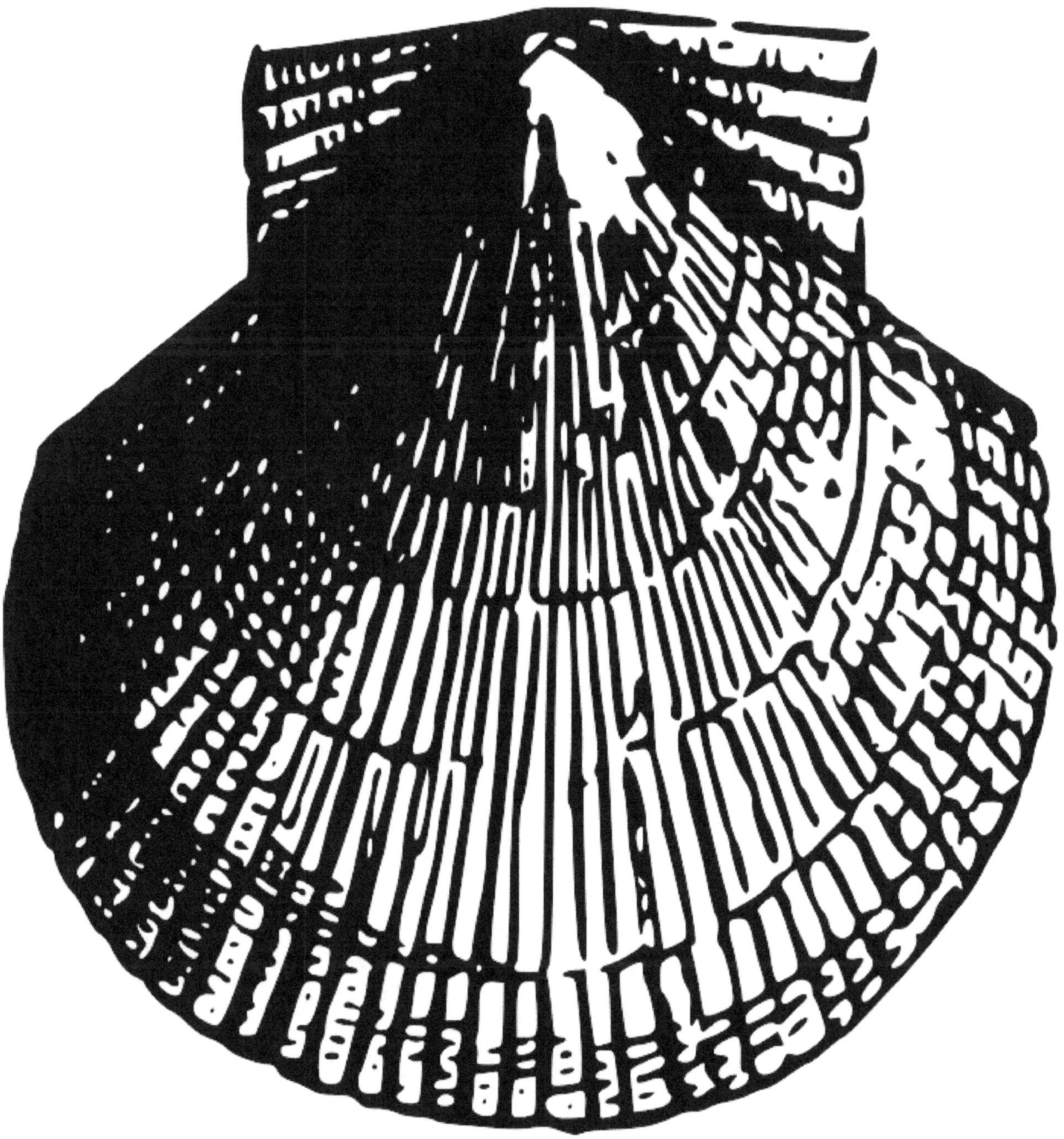

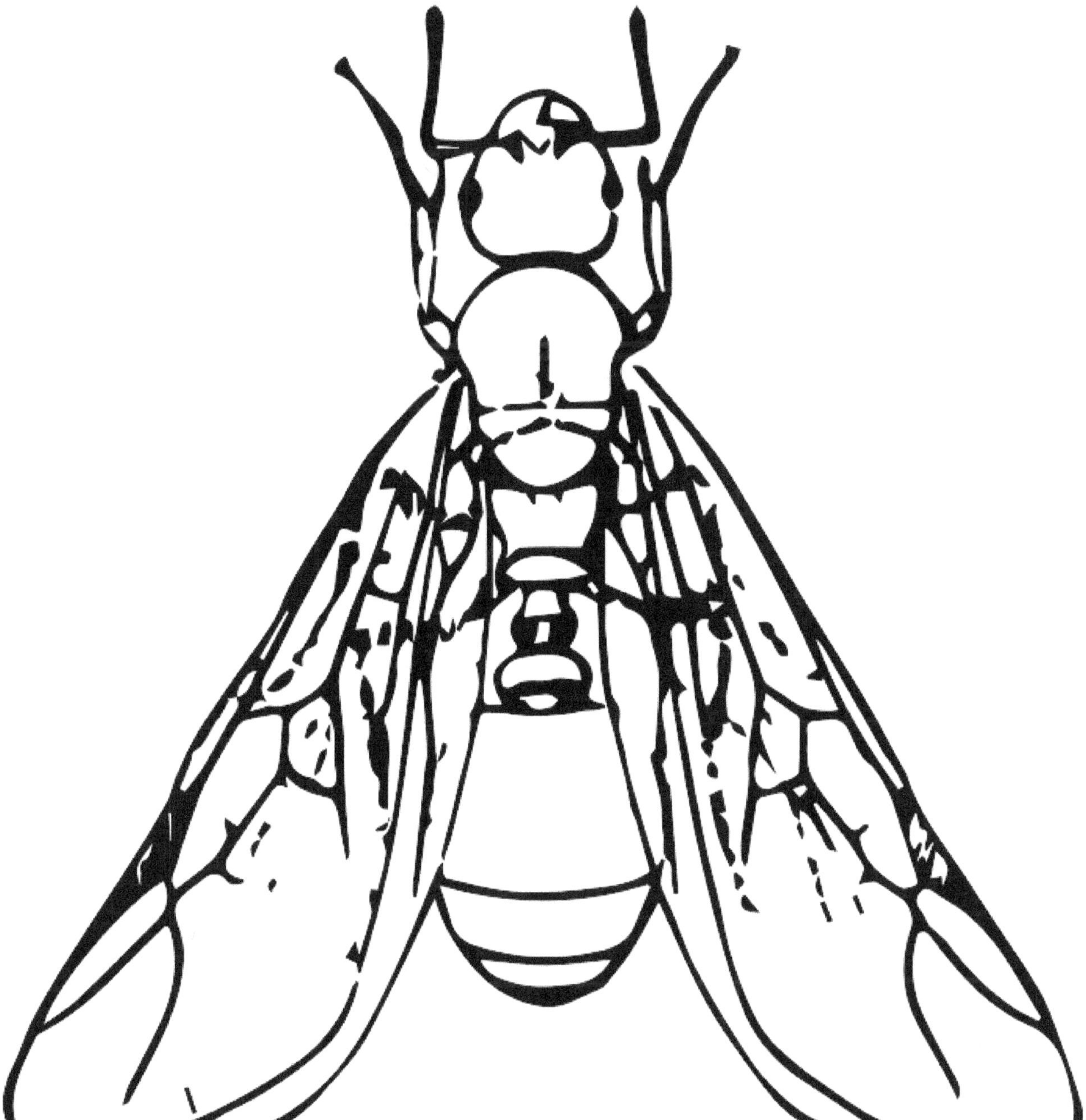

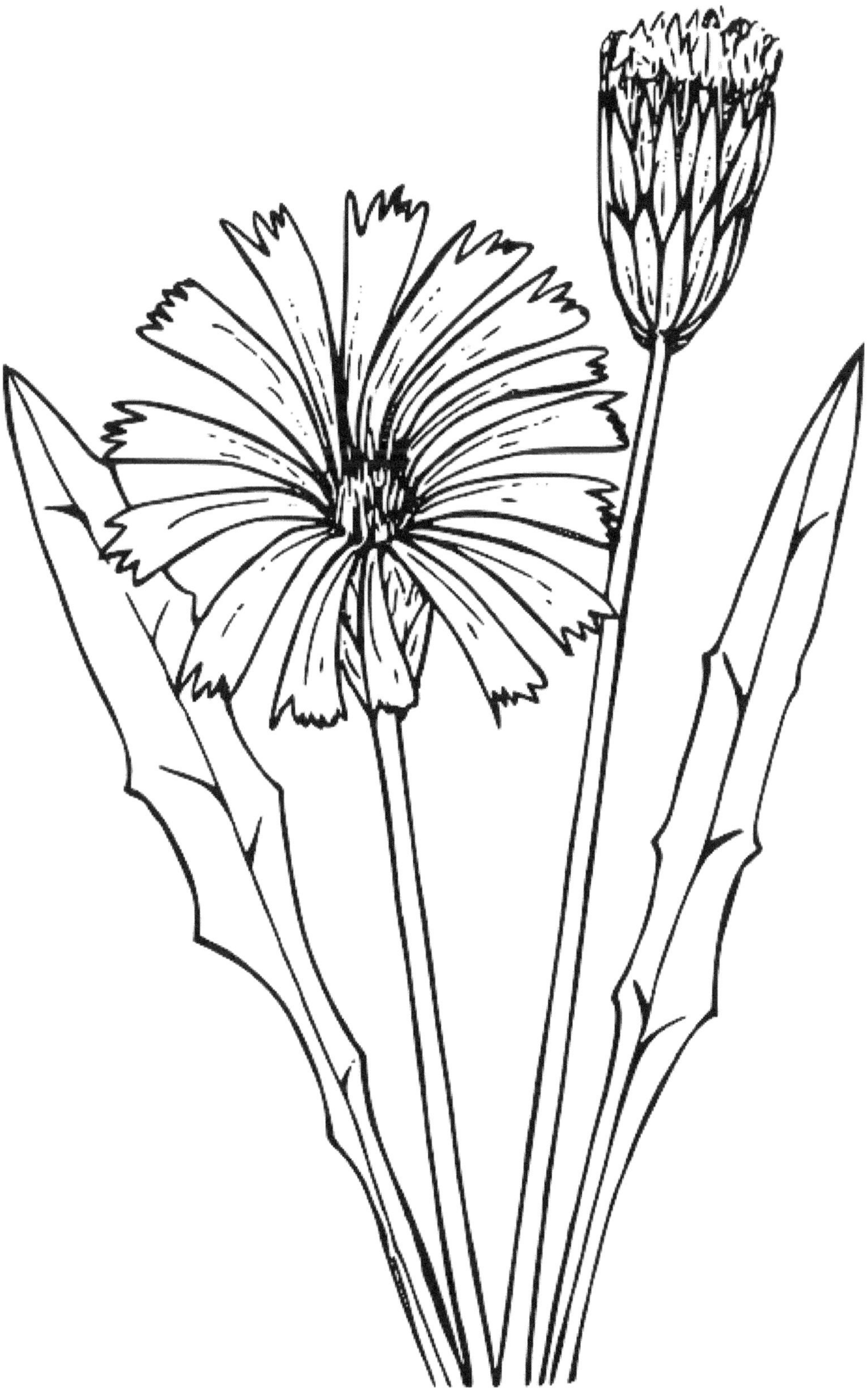

Enjoy even more *Colouring Books for Grown-Ups,* including:

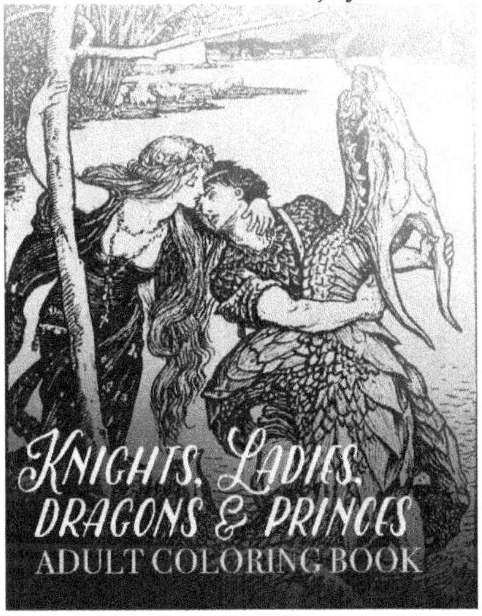

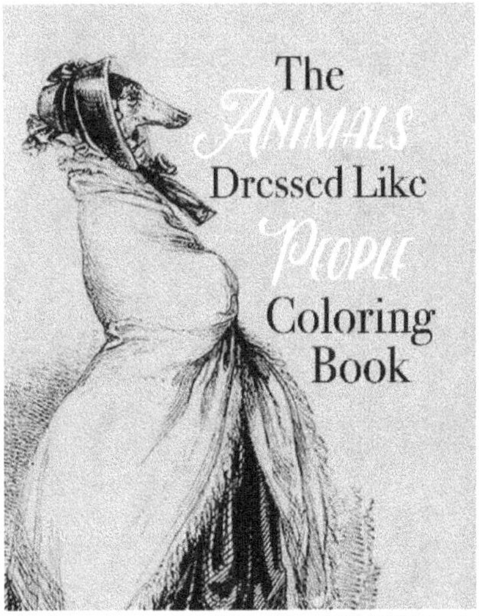

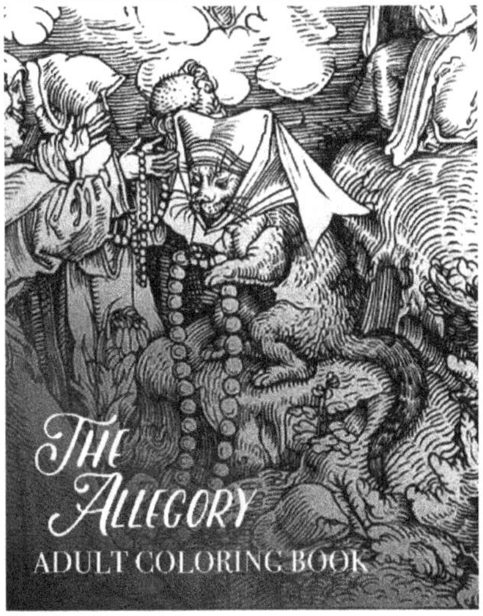

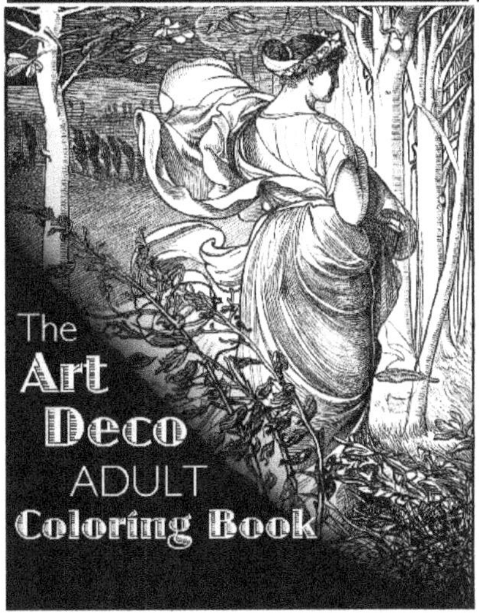

www.ingramcontent.com/pod-product-compliance
Lightning Source LLC
Chambersburg PA
CBHW081754280526
45789CB00008B/2853